THE WACKY, WEIRD & WONDERFUL NOVELTY SONGBOOK

Project Manager: Carol Cuellar
Song Contributor: Sy Feldman
Art Layout: Ken Rehm

CONTENTS

THE ABA DABA HONEYMOON

Words and Music by
ARTHUR FIELDS and
WALTER DONOVAN

AHAB, THE ARAB

Words and Music by
RAY STEVENS

Let me tell you 'bout A - hab, the A - rab, The sheik of the burn - ing sand. He had em'-ralds and ru - bies just a -drip -ping off of him. And a

ring on ev - 'ry fin - ger of his hands. He wore a

big old tur - ban wrapped a - round his head And a

scim - i - tar by his side ___ And ev - 'ry eve - ning a - bout

mid - night He'd jump on his cam - el named Clyde ___

Spoken:
and ride through the night to the Sultan's tent where he would secretly meet up with Fatima of the seven veils, the swingingest number one dancer in the Sultan's whole harem, 'cause like him and her had a thing going. You know, they'd been carrying on for some time now behind the Sultan's back and you could hear him talk to his camel. As he rode out across the dunes, his voice would cut through the still night desert air and he'd say, (imitate Arabian speech) which is Arabic for, "Woa, babies." And Clyde would say, (imitate camel voice). Well, he

brought his camel to a screeching halt at the rear of Fatima's tent, jumped off Clyde, snook around the corner and into the tent he went. There he saw Fatima lying on a zebra skin rug, wearing rings on her fingers and bells on her toes and a bone in her nose. Ho, ho.

There she was, friends and neighbors, lying there in all her radiant beauty, eating on a raisin and a grape and an apricot and a pomegranate and a bowl of chitterlings, two bananas, three Hershey bars, and sipping an R-ER-C coke cola, listening to her transistor, watching The Grand Old Opry and reading Mad Magazine while she sang, "Does you chewing gum lose its flavor?" And Ahab walked up to her and he said, (imitate Arabian speech) which is Arabic for, "Let's twist again like we did last summer, babies." And she said, (coy, girlish laugh) "Crazy baby." 'Round and around and around and around, etc. And that's the story 'bout

A - hab, the A - rab, The sheik of the burn - ing sand. __

ALEXANDER'S RAGTIME BAND

Words and Music by
IRVING BERLIN

ALL I WANT FOR CHRISTMAS IS
MY TWO FRONT TEETH

Words and Music by
DON GARDNER

THE BABBIT AND THE BROMIDE

Music and Lyrics by
GEORGE GERSHWIN and IRA GERSHWIN

15

BABY SITTIN' BOOGIE

Moderate Boogie Tempo

Words and Music by
JOHNNY PARKER

(Coos, gurgles and any sort of baby sounds -) My
Girl version: When

girl _____ ba - by sits for some - one on her block, _____ then
I _____ ba - by sit for some - one on my block, _____ my

I come up and join her and we start to rock. _ The ba - by hears the beat and, man, it
guy comes up and joins me and we start to rock. _

is a shock _ when he goes (Baby sounds - - - - - - - - -) A { rock - in' type of boog - ie is the
know there is - n't an - y - one to

Optional - - - - - - - - - - - - - -

BARNEY GOOGLE

Words and Music by
BILLY ROSE and CON CONRAD

BE MY LITTLE BABY BUMBLEBEE

Words by STANLEY MURPHY
Music by HENRY I. MARSHALL

BOTTLE OF WINE

Words and Music by
TOM PAXTON

Chorus: Bot - tle Of Wine, fruit of the vine, When you gon - na let me get so - ber? Leave me a - lone, let me go home, Let me go back and start o - ver. o - ver.

Verse: 1. Ram - bl - in' 'round this dirt - y old town, Sing - in' for nick - els and dimes. ___ Times get - tin' rough, I ain't got e - nough to get a lit - tle Bot - tle Of Wine.

2. Pain in my head, bugs in my bed,
Pants are so old that they shine.
Out on the street, tell the people I meet,
Buy me a bottle of wine.
(Chorus)

3. Preacher will preach, teacher will teach,
Miner will dig in the mine,
I ride the rods, trusting in God,
Huggin' my bottle of wine.
(Chorus)

BLAH-BLAH-BLAH

Music and Lyrics by
GEORGE GERSHWIN and IRA GERSHWIN

Moderato

writ-ten you a song, A beau-ti-ful rou-tine; (I hope you

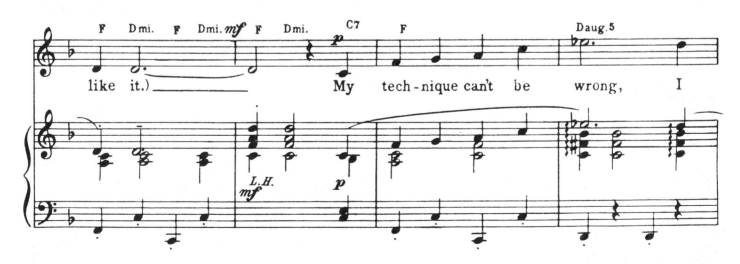

like it.) My tech-nique can't be wrong, I

CEMENT MIXER
(Put-Ti, Put-Ti)

Words and Music by
SLIM GAILLARD and LEE RICKS

THE CHICKEN DANCE
(a.k.a. Dance Little Bird)

By TERRY RENDALL and
WERNER THOMAS
English Lyric by
PAUL PARNES

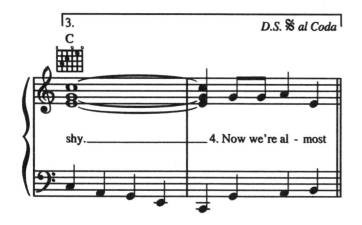

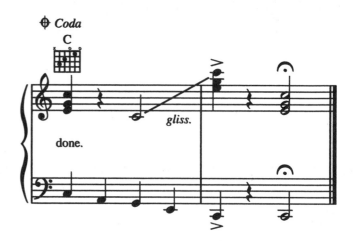

Verse 2:
Hey, you're in the swing.
You're cluckin' like a bird. (Pluck, pluck, pluck, pluck.)
You're flappin' your wings.
Don't you feel absurd. (No, no, no, no.)
It's a chicken dance,
Like a rooster and a hen. (Ya, ya, ya, ya.)
Flappy chicken dance;
Let's do it again. *(To Chorus 2:)*

Chorus 2:
Relax and let the music move you.
Let all your inhibitions go.
Just watch your partner whirl around you.
We're havin' fun now; I told you so.

Verse 3:
Now you're flappin' like a bird
And you're wigglin' too. (I like that move.)
You're without a care.
It's a dance for you. (Just made for you.)
Keep doin' what you do.
Don't you cop out now. (Don't cop out now.)
Gets better as you dance;
Catch your breath somehow. *(To Chorus 3:)*

Verse 4:
Now we're almost through,
Really flyin' high. (Bye, bye, bye, bye.)
All you chickens and birds,
Time to say goodbye. (To say goodbye.)
Goin' back to the nest,
But the flyin' was fun. (Oh, it was fun.)
Chicken dance was the best,
But the dance is done.

CHINATOWN, MY CHINATOWN

Words by
WILLIAM JEROME

Words by WILLIAM JEROME
Music by JEAN SCHWARTZ

A CUP OF COFFEE, A SANDWICH AND YOU

Words by BILLY ROSE and AL DUBIN
Music by JOSEPH MEYER

39

DOES YOUR CHEWING GUM LOSE ITS FLAVOR ON THE BEDPOST OVER NIGHT?

(Does the Spearmint Lose Its Flavor on the Bedpost Overnight?)

Words and Music by
BILLY ROSE, MARTY BLOOM and ERNEST BREVER

Chorus

"yes" or is it "no"
volves the con - ti - nent"
choir be - gins to sing:
}
*"Does The Spear-mint Lose Its Flav - or On The Bed - post O - ver

Night?
{
If you chew it in the morn - ing will it be too hard to
If you pull it out like rub - ber will it snap right back and
Would you use it on your col - lar when your but - ton's not in

bite? Can't you see I'm go - ing craz - y, won't some - bod - y put me right?
bite? If you paste it on the left side, will you find it on the right?
sight? Put your hand be - neath your left seat and you will find it there all right?
}
*"Does The

Spear - mint Lose Its Flav - or On The Bed - post O - ver Night?" *"Does The Night?"___

D.S. al Coda

*Alternate line "Does Your Chewing Gum Lose etc. . . .

DOIN' THE PIGEON

Words and Music by
JOE RAPOSO
Arranged by MARTY GOLD

DOODLE DOO DOO

Words and Music by
ART KASSEL and MEL STITZEL

ESCAPE
(The Piña Colada Song)

Words and Music by
RUPERT HOLMES

HANDS UP
(Give Me Your Heart)

Original Words and Music by
JEAN KLUGER and DANIEL VANGARDE
English Adaptation by
NELLIE BYL

Hands up, ba-by, hands up. Give me your heart, give me, give me your heart, give it, give it,

Hands up, ba-by, hands up. Give me your heart, give me, give me your heart, give it, give it,

HAPPY FEET

Words by JACK YELLEN
Music by MILTON AGER

to my shoes   Be-cause my shoes re - fuse   to ev - er grow

wear - y.   I keep cheer-ful   on an ear-ful

of mus - ic sweet,___   'Cause I've got   hap - hap - hap - py

feet.   feet.___

HELLO MUDDAH, HELLO FADDAH!
(A Letter From Camp)

Words by ALLAN SHERMAN
Music by LOU BUSCH

62

min-ute, it stopped hail-ing. Guys are swim-ming, guys are

sail-ing! Play-ing base-ball, gee that's bet - ter. Mud-dah,

fad - duh, kind - ly dis - re - gard this let - ter.

Hel - lo let - ter.

HARD HEARTED HANNAH
(The Vamp of Savannah)

Words and Music by
JACK YELLEN, MILTON AGER,
BOB BIGELOW and CHARLES BATES

65

HINKY DINKY PARLEY-VOO

TRADITIONAL

HOORAY FOR CAPTAIN SPAULDING

Words and Music by
BERT KALMAR and HARRY RUBY

I LOVE A PIANO

Words and Music by
IRVING BERLIN

HYMN FOR A SUNDAY EVENING
(Ed Sullivan)

Words by LEE ADAMS
Music by CHARLES STROUSE

IF I ONLY HAD A BRAIN

Lyrics by E.Y. HARBURG
Music by HAROLD ARLEN

I could while a-way the hours con - ferr - in' with the flow'rs con -
When a man's an emp - ty ket - tle he should be on his met - tle and

sult - in' with the rain_____ And my
yet I'm torn a - part_____ Just be -

IF ANIMALS HAD NEVER BEEN INVENTED

Words by JUDY SPENCER
Music by EARL ROSE

85

I'M A ZOO

Words and Music by
JUDY SPENCER and EARL ROSE

JAVA JIVE

Words by MILTON DRAKE
Music by BEN OAKLAND

INTERLUDE

JEEPERS CREEPERS

Words by JOHNNY MERCER
Music by HARRY WARREN

JOHNNY ONE NOTE

Words by LORENZ HART
Music by RICHARD RODGERS

LESBIAN SEAGULL

Words and Music by
TOM WILSON WEINBERG

Verse 2:
She skims the water at their mealtime to seek
A fish, and she emerges with one squirming in her beak.
She plays among the waves and hides between the swells,
She walks the beach at twilight, searching for some shells.
(To Chorus:)

Verse 3:
And in the evening, as they watch the setting sun,
She looks to her as if to say, "The day is done."
It's time to find their shelter hidden in the dunes,
And fall asleep amidst the music of the loons.

Chorus 3:
You and me, lesbian seagull,
We'll just watch the world go by.
Just you and me, lesbian seagull,
Side be side we'll be till we die.
You and I, we can make it if we try.
Our love will keep us flying high until we die.

LYDIA, THE TATTOOED LADY

Music by HAROLD ARLEN
Lyric by E.Y. HARBURG

109

LITTLE SIR ECHO

Original Version by
LAURA R. SMITH and J.S. FEARIS
Words and Revised Arrangement by
ADELE GIRARD and JOE MARSALA

Moderate Waltz

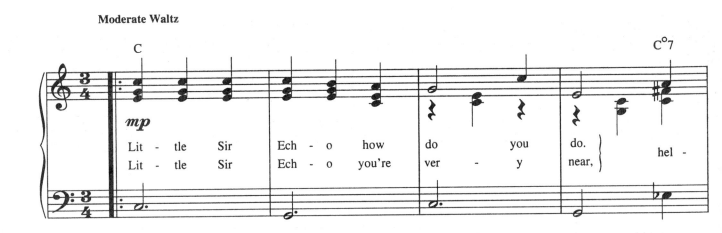

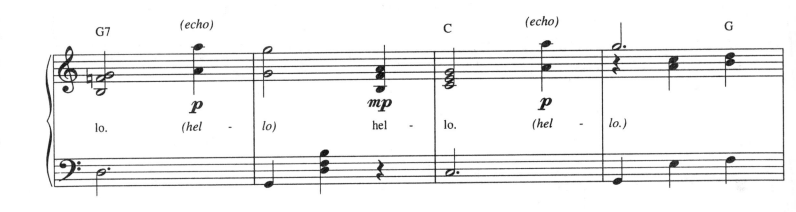

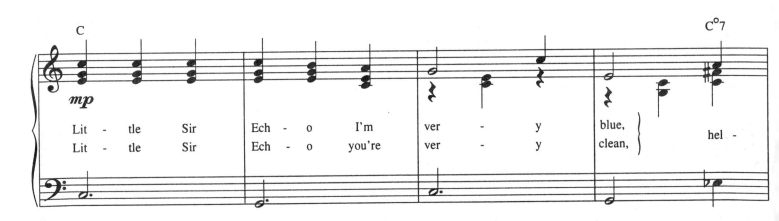

MACARENA

Words and Music by
ANTONIO ROMERO and RAFAEL RUIZ

Coro:

Da - le a tu cuer - po a-le - grí - a Ma-ca - re-na que tu cuer-po es pa' dar - le a-le - grí-a y co-sa bue-na.

Da - le a tu cuer - po a - le - grí - a Ma - ca - re - na,   eh,_____ Ma - ca - re - na.

Verso 3:
Macarena sueña con el Corte inglés
Y se compra los modelos mas modernos.
Le gustaría vivir en Nueva York
Y ligar un novio nuevo.

Puente 2:
Macarena sueña con el Corte inglés
Y se compra los modelos mas modernos.
Le gustaría vivir en Nueva York
Y ligar un novio nuevo.
(Al Coro:)

Verso 4:
Macarena tiene un novio que se llama,
Que se llama de apellido Vitorino.
Y en la jura de bandera del muchacho
Se la dió con dos amigos.

Puente 3:
Macarena tiene un novio que se llama,
Que se llama de apellido Vitorino.
Y en la jura de bandera del muchacho
Se la dió con dos amigos.
(Al Coro:)

MAIRZY DOATS

Words and Music by
MILTON DRAKE, AL HOFFMAN
and JERRY LIVINGSTON

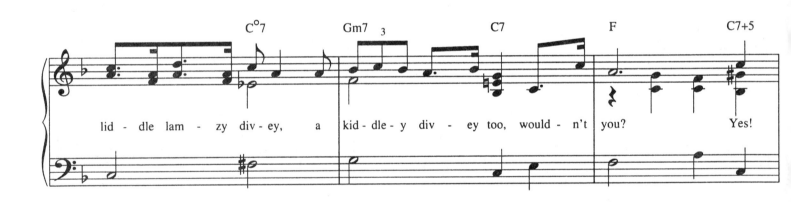

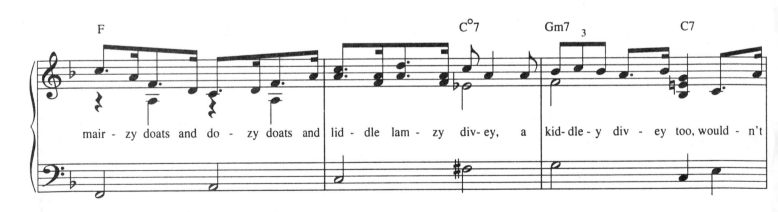

MAKE 'EM LAUGH

Words by ARTHUR FREED
Music by NACIO HERB BROWN

Make 'em roar, make 'em scream,
Don't you know all the world wants to laugh?
My Grandpa said,"Go out and tell 'em a joke,
But give it plenty of hoke."
Make 'em roar, make 'em scream,
Take a fall, butt a wall, split a seam.
You start off by pretending you're a dancer with grace,
You wiggle till they're giggling all over the place,
And then you get a great big custard pie in the face,
Make 'em laugh, make 'em laugh, make 'em laugh!

MINNIE, THE MOOCHER

Words and Music by
CAB CALLOWAY and IRVING MILLS

Chorus

MISCHA, YASCHA, TOSCHA, SASCHA

Music and Lyrics by
GEORGE GERSHWIN and ARTHUR FRANCIS

Refrain:

Temp-r'a- men - tal O - ri - en - tal Gen-tle-men are we,

Mis - cha Yas - cha, Tos - cha Sas - cha, Fid-dle le fid-dle le dee.

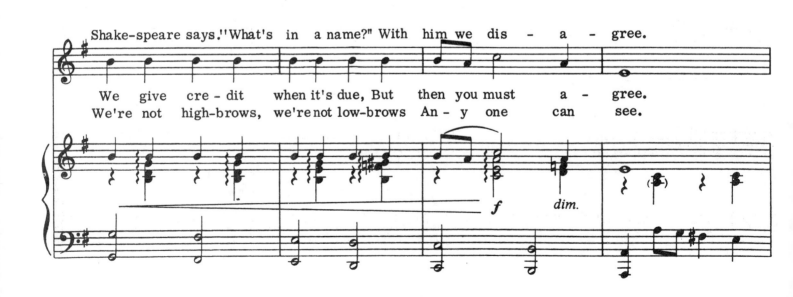

Shake-speare says. "What's in a name?" With him we dis - a - gree.

We give cre - dit when it's due, But then you must a - gree.
We're not high-brows, we're not low-brows An - y one can see.

MOSES

Words by BETTY COMDEN and ADOLPH GREEN
Music by ROGER EDENS

OCTOPUS'S GARDEN

Words and Music by
RICHARD STARKEY

136

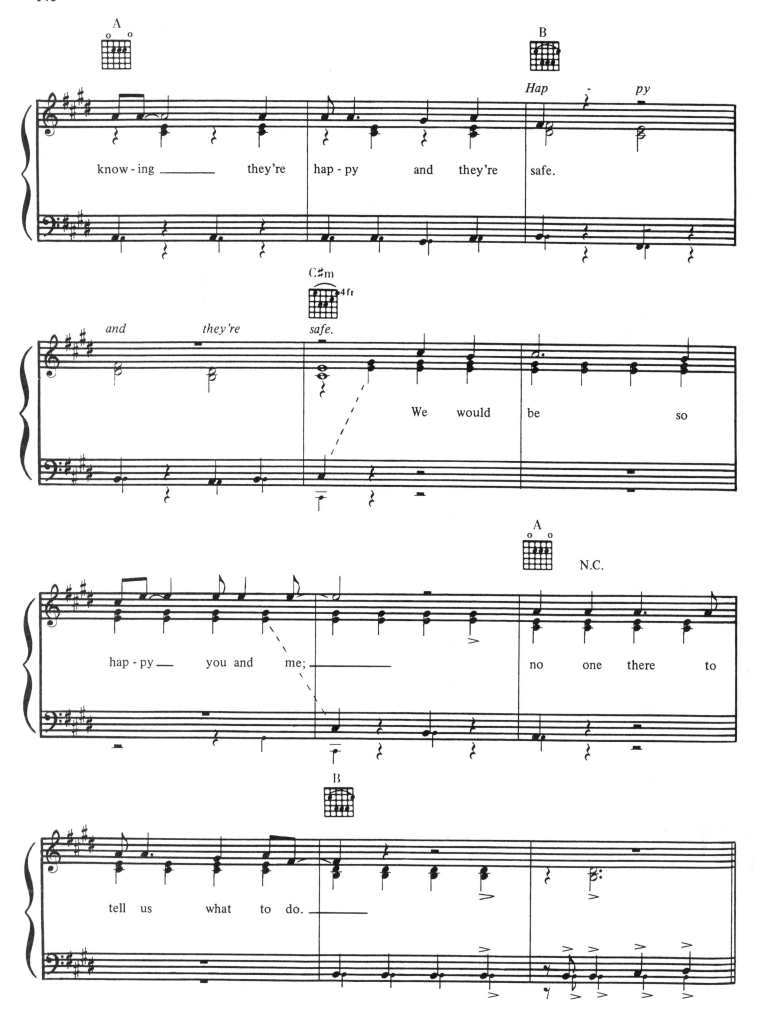

PASS THAT PEACE PIPE

Words and Music by
ROGER EDENS, HUGH MARTIN
and RALPH BLANE

PUFF (THE MAGIC DRAGON)

Words and Music by
PETER YARROW and LEONARD LIPTON

SUGGESTED GUITAR STRUM

Peter uses Travis picking to accompany this song. Be sure to
capo up two frets in order to be in the same key as the record.

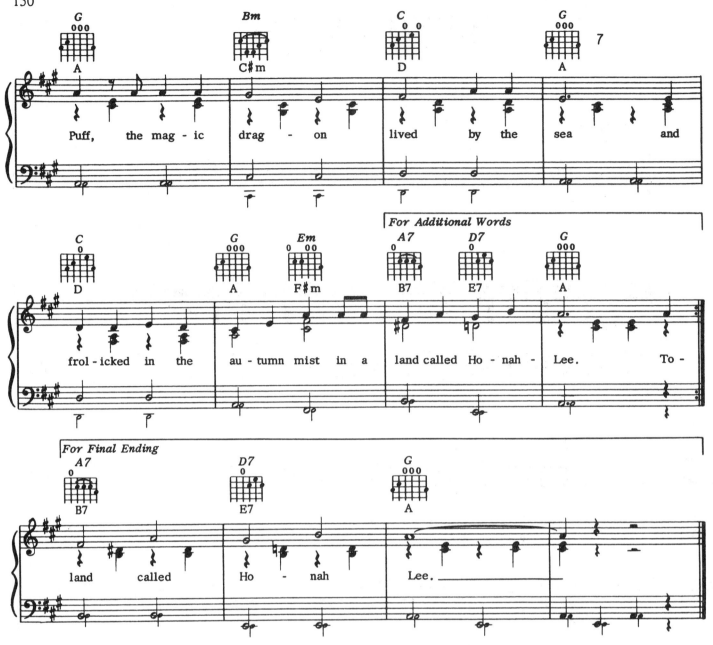

ADDITIONAL WORDS

2. Together they would travel on a boat with billowed sail,
   Jackie kept a lookout perched on Puff's gigantic tail,
   Noble kings and princes would bow whene'er they came,
   Pirate ships would low'r their flag when Puff roared out his name. Oh!
   (Chorus)

3. A dragon lives forever but not so little boys,
   Painted wings and giant rings make way for other toys.
   One grey night it happened, Jackie Paper came no more
   And Puff that mighty dragon, he ceased his fearless roar. Oh!
   (Chorus)

4. His head was bent in sorrow, green scales fell like rain,
   Puff no longer went to play along the cherry lane.
   Without his life-long friend, Puff could not be brave
   So Puff that mighty dragon, sadly slipped into his cave. Oh!
   (Chorus)

SCHNITZELBANK

Lyrics by RANDY ROGEL
TRADITIONAL

152

spoken: (Are we having fun yet?)   cuck-oo clock,   tick tick tock,   piece of chalk,   key and lock.

Oh, du schoe-ne,   oh, du schoe-ne   oh, du schoe-ne schnitz-el-bank!   *(talk)*

(1st voice(s))   *(2nd voice(s))*

1. Is das nicht ein   piece of bread?   Ya das ist ein   piece of bread.   Does it fit in   Wak-kos head?
2. Is he not a   cute man this?   Ya he is a   cute man this.   Is this not a   great big kiss?

A QUAKE! A QUAKE!

Music and Lyrics by
RANDY ROGEL

while the ground moves a - round. We won't let it get us down. Get be-neath the

door frame. A quake, a quake, it's time to pull up

(voice(s) 1.)   *(voice(s) 2.)*

stake. The worst is o - ver, we don't buy it. We're fed up, we can't de - ny it.

We just want some peace and qui - et____ so we're mov - ing to Bei - rut.

SHE LIKES BASKETBALL

Words by HAL DAVID
Music by BURT BACHARACH

SEVEN LITTLE GIRLS SITTING
IN THE BACK SEAT

Words by BOB HILLIARD
Music by LEE POCKRISS

THE SONG'S GOTTA COME FROM THE HEART

Lyric by SAMMY CAHN
Music by JULE STYNE

SOUTH AMERICA, TAKE IT AWAY

Words and Music by
HAROLD ROME

THE THING

Words and Music by
CHARLES R. GREAN

3) I turned around and got right out a-runnin' for my life,
And then I took it home with me to give it to my wife.
But this is what she hollered at me as I walked in the door:
Oh, get out of here with that xxx and don't come back no more.
Oh, get out of here with that xxx and don't come back no more.

4) I wandered all around the town until I chanced to meet
A hobo who was looking for a handout on the street.
He said he'd take most any old thing, he was a desperate man,
But when I showed him the xxx, he turned around and ran.
Oh, when I showed him the xxx, he turned around and ran.

5) I wandered on for many years, a victim of my fate,
Until one day I came upon Saint Peter at the gate.
And when I tried to take it inside he told me where to go:
Get out of here with that xxx and take it down below.
Oh, get out of here with that xxx and take it down below.

6) The moral of the story is if you're out on the beach
And you should see a great big box and it's within your reach,
Don't ever stop and open it up, that's my advice to you,
'Cause you'll never get rid of the xxx, no matter what you do.
Oh, you'll never get rid of the xxx, no matter what you do.

THE VARSITY DRAG

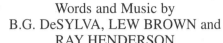

Words and Music by
B.G. DeSYLVA, LEW BROWN and
RAY HENDERSON

Lyrics:
We've al - ways thought, know - ledge___ is naught; We should be taught to dance. Right here at Tait, We're up___ to date; We teach a great new

Refrain *(brightly)*

Here is the Drag, See how it goes; Down on the heels, up on the toes.

That's the way to do the Var - si - ty Drag._____

Hot - ter than hot, New - er than new! Mean - er than mean, Blu - er than blue,

Gets as much ap - plause as wav - ing the Flag!

WHEN BANANA SKINS ARE FALLING
(I'll Come Sliding Back To You)

Words and Music by
A. FRAZZINI, PAUL DeFRANK
and IRVING MILLS

Got a job out on a farm just a gar-den and a barn,

Ev - er since I went a - way I've been lone-some night and day,

UNDER THE BAMBOO TREE

Music by ROSAMOND JOHNSON
Words by BOB COLE

YAKKO'S WORLD

Lyrics by
RANDY ROGEL
TRADITIONAL

MANAGUA, NICARAGUA

Lyric by ALBERT GAMSE
Music by IRVING FIELDS

Won't you kind-ly op-en your ge-o-gra-phy __ Let us turn to page one hun-dred twen-ty three __ Be-tween the Car-ib-bean and the Pa-cif-ic shore You'll find a ci-ty of "A-mor." MA - NA-GUA, NI-CA-RA-GUA is a beau-ti-ful town, You

80 Years of Popular Music

This brilliant new series from Warner Bros. Publications collects the biggest singles and sheet music sellers for each decade. Each book contains:
- **Exciting colorful covers** • **Dozens of #1 and Top 10 hit songs**
- **The best artists and best music ever** **A special historical overview of each decade** • **Great price**

The whole series makes great collectibles and contains music your customers already know and love. They'll use these books year after year. Stock up today!!!

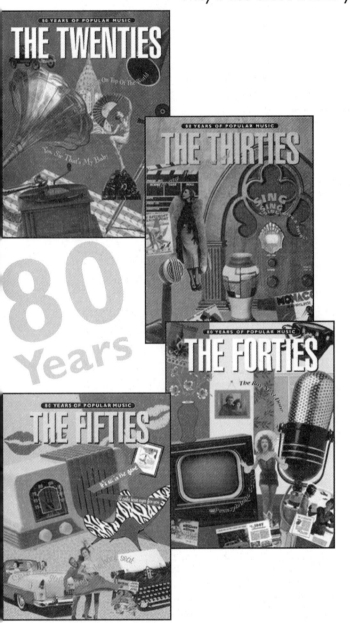

The Thirties

Piano/Vocal/Chords
(MF9824)
ISBN 0-7692-6722-X UPC 0-29156-95403-6

Titles in this 47-song collection include: **Anything Goes • As Time Goes By • Begin the Beguine • Blue Moon • Brother Can You Spare a Dime • For All We Know • Hooray for Hollywood • I Got Rhythm • I Only Have Eyes for You • It Don't Mean a Thing (If It Ain't Got That Swing) • It's Only a Paper Moon • I'm in the Mood for Love • Mood Indigo • Over the Rainbow • Sophisticated Lady • Stars Fell on Alabama • You and the Night and the Music** and more.

The Forties

Piano/Vocal/Chords
(MF9825)
ISBN 0-7692-6723-8 UPC 0-29156-95404-3

Titles in this 57-song collection include: **Autumn Serenade • Blues in the Night • Chattanooga Choo Choo • Don't Fence Me In • Don't Get Around Much Anymore • Don't Sit Under the Apple Tree (With Anyone Else But Me) • Fools Rush In • I Got It Bad and That Ain't Good • I'll Walk Alone • Laura • New York, New York • Pennsylvania 6-5000 • Rum and Coca-Cola • Shangri-La • Two O'Clock Jump • You Stepped Out of a Dream** and more.

The Fifties

Piano/Vocal/Chords
(MF9826)
ISBN 0-7692-6724-6 UPC 0-29156-95405-0

Titles in this 72-song collection include: **All I Have to Do is Dream • Be-Bop-A-Lula • Bye Bye, Love • Catch a Falling Star • Chantilly Lace • Earth Angel • Good Golly Miss Molly • I Only Have Eyes for You • I'm Walkin' • La Bamba • Let the Good Times Roll • The Lion Sleeps Tonight (Wimoweh) • Lonely Boy • My Boy Lollipop • (We're Gonna) Rock Around the Clock • Shout • Splish Splash • Teen Angel • Wake Up Little Susie • Why Do Fools Fall in Love • Your Cheatin' Heart** and more.

The Twenties

Piano/Vocal/Chords
(MF9823)
ISBN 0-7692-6721-1 UPC 0-29156-95402-9

Titles in this 52-song collection include: **Ain't Misbehavin' • Ain't She Sweet • Bye Bye Blackbird • Charleston • Five Foot Two, Eyes of Blue • Happy Days Are Here Again • Ida, Sweet As Apple Cider • If You Knew Susie (Like I Knew Susie) • I'm Just Wild About Harry • I'm Sitting on Top of the World • Love Me or Leave Me • Makin' Whoopee! • My Blue Heaven • Someone to Watch Over Me • Sweet Georgia Brown • Tea for Two • When You're Smiling** and more.

AD0153

80 80
Years of Popular
Music

The Sixties

Piano/Vocal/Chords
(MF9827)
ISBN 0-7692-6725-4 UPC 0-29156-95406-7

Titles in this 82-song collection include: **Aquarius/Let the Sun Shine In • Bad Moon Rising • California Girls • (Sittin' On) The Dock of the Bay • The House of the Rising Sun • I Got You Babe • I Saw Her Standing There • In-A-Gadda-Da-Vida • Itsy Bitsy Teeny Weenie Yellow Polka Dot Bikini • Mony, Mony • Oh, Pretty Woman • Raindrops Keep Fallin' on My Head • Soul Man • When a Man Loves a Woman • White Rabbit • Wipe Out** and more.

The Seventies

Piano/Vocal/Chords
(MF9828)
ISBN 0-7692-6985-0 UPC 0-29156-95704-4

Titles in this 58-song collection include: **Baby I Love Your Way • Didn't I Blow Your Mind This Time • Go Your Own Way • A Horse with No Name • Hotel California • If You Don't Know Me By Now • I'll Take You There • Killing Me Softly with His Song • Love Train • My Sharona • Old Time Rock & Roll • The Rose • Stairway to Heaven • Time in a Bottle • What a Fool Believes • You Are So Beautiful** and more.

The Eighties

Piano/Vocal/Chords
(MF9829)
ISBN 0-7692-6994-X UPC 0-29156-95742-6

Titles in this 55-song collection include: **Africa • Against All Odds (Take a Look at Me Now) • Arthur's Theme (Best That You Can Do) • Back in the High Life Again • Cuts Like a Knife • I Will Always Love You • In the Air Tonight • Like a Rock • Man in the Mirror • On the Wings of Love • (I've Had) The Time of My Life • Up Where We Belong • What's Love Got to Do with It • Words Get in the Way** and more.

The Nineties

Piano/Vocal/Chords
(MF9830)
ISBN 0-7692-7103-0 UPC 0-29156-95950-5

Titles in this 58-song collection include: **All I Wanna Do • All My Life • Because You Loved Me • Foolish Games • I Believe I Can Fly • (Everything I Do) I Do It for You • I Don't Want to Miss a Thing • I Love You Always Forever • I Swear • I'll Be There for You (Theme from "Friends") • Kiss from a Rose • MMMBop • Quit Playing Games with My Heart • Sunny Came Home • Tears in Heaven • Un-Break My Heart • Walking on the Sun • You're Still the One** and more.